WARPAINT ANGEL

Warpaint Angel

Robert Hamberger

10·9·97

For
my dear friend Jackie
you keep me going!
With all my love
Rob
xxx

BLACKWATER
P R E S S

First Published in United Kingdom in 1997
by
Blackwater Press
17 Holbrook Road, Leicester LE2 3LG
England

Printed in England by
Leighton Printing Company
London N7 8DH

© Robert Hamberger

A CIP catalogue record for this book is available from the British
Library.

ISBN 0 9528557 1 2

for

Seth and Louis and Lily

CONTENTS

ACTS OF THE FATHER

WARPAINT ANGEL

Now God help thee, poor monkey!
But how wilt thou do for a father?
                              Macbeth (Act 4 Scene2)

A man becomes old photographs.

He left, years after   died
                        I can't begin.

Air bubbles stipple like rain
across a lake apparently calm two minutes ago
dredging, with last year's leaves
shoulders
a face
a stubble-rough laugh.
While light drowses the afternoon
we turn to each other.
He's been here all this time,
waiting to be admitted
like a guest treading dust under the elms.

                        Acts of the father:
he thumbed mud along my forehead
over my cheeks,
warpaint angel with a dirty face
a wire halo, crepe-paper dress.
If we talked late he was angry,
we must kneel beside the bed
- a stick in his fist swings down.
"And this" he said one Christmas
drawing aside the yellow bedroom curtain
"is the best present of all":
shreds of the white sky flickering
the finest snow.
I've never got away from that cold.
Stubborn icicle   it won't dissolve
drizzling these visions to the end of a narrow point.

Violence and tenderness   acts of the father
printed on our skin like holy law
unquestioned   what made him tick?

The mystery ritual
a scene I shoot from every angle
threading, unthreading   the day he left.

A man a woman three children
divide,
either walk outside to the car
or return to a room that seems to be no different.
There's only more space in the mirror
two jackets gone from the chair.

I take it like a man   the simple speech
where their mouths mime in unison
and their voices can't quite match:
"Wedding bells stop in the air.
We couldn't understand the people we'd become
the people we've become no longer love.
You'll count as many reasons as leaves on a tree
why wedding bells stop in the air."
Sometimes I remember it as silence
in slow motion
bleaching towards the sun.

The last time
I hid from his visit,
bunched like a fist inside the broken roundabout.
He wavered between the gates and saw
a football roll to a slowing stop
while a boy pretends he isn't here.

One page of paper torn in half
                    we recovered
hugging others like a shipwreck
eighteen years
                    until he died.

Tonight
after rain
I windowshop for ghosts,
spit and glue a papier-maché mask
the colour of newsprint, a photograph grin
try it on for size and call it father.
He shrank: a stoppered genie
unappeased.
One morning he'll balloon from the kettle-spout,
fold his arms, answer every unachieved desire.
Breath's not enough   the magic word snares in my throat.

For years I've been starting
to father husband searchlight myself,
revolve revolve our relationship
as a glass twists in the sun.
Two people miss each other's message
evade or leave, and no chance to explain.

I stash his piecemeal legacy:
casual snapshots, the repertoire of moves.
He was kind   he had a temper
I hardly knew him
valued as the father, no-one else
with no childhood, allegiances, views of his own.
Bones guzzled by a winter fox.

He's only a father
the power is limited.
He was only a man,
balancing the need to love
with techniques honed for survival,
working out the day his son takes over
all he has to give:
tightened veins on a clenched hand
the rough, embarrassed kiss
constricted voice, and bitter incantation
you won't feel you won't feel a thing.

Malice   compassion
these mending beliefs
might resolve any moment
like an answer in the mouth

to face him   at last   as an equal.

I dream of meetings:
the grand reconciliation,
holding you, weeping
as a father would a child.
The dream is you would love me,
heal me like a laying on of hands
                    you're nowhere
these hands are only mine,
almost gentle as a man's
against my face
against my closing eyes.

ADAM AND THE THIRD SON

And Adam knew his wife again; and she bare a son,
and called his name Seth: For God, said she, hath
appointed me another seed instead of Abel, whom
Cain slew.

Genesis Chapter 4 Verse 25.

Adam speaks to Seth, his newborn son:

My prayer drips to land stiff as honeycomb
where thistles fester
and the belly of a serpent slurs its chain.
You're the epilogue for every risk that's left me
wheezing to a child about old times.
Once I sprawled this kingdom spitting pips
while every knot of breath and blood
became the name I gave it.
God nicked a rib, made a woman rise like bread:
he said it would be so.

After the nibbled apple
thumped to feed the grass
God barged around his garden
like a querulous dad.
Innocence slushed in the bucket.
It pocked and clunked, a hollow ring,
five days walk from Eden.
Nothing buds here,
only the rooted cries of sons
plucked from your mother's bed.

The message
from your brothers
is blood.
It scuds over the topsoil
sluiced by puddling rain,
it bubbles and it cannot rinse away.
Power nailed the blade into your brother
power and its sister death
one hand each
split his eggshell ribs.

God stung me blind.
He bribed his boy with paradise
built on knowing nothing.
This itch to rule, compete, control,
surged like lilac through God's plot:
a drenched, deceptive scent
blossoms over one son's punctured skin.
My life is weakened snow now,
my veins are fidgety rivers
loosening ice.

Your milk breath
heals the withered season,
turns your stooping parents to the sun.
We can't command when you wet, when you wake
have no say
in the seeds you'll crop without us.
Learn from the losses of the first three men:
begin a tender breed,
when rivalry dives in the ocean
and power's less important than the peach that holds a stone.

THE MAN WHO HITS THE DANCING BEAR
(Rajasthan)

I'm his father,
trained him from a fur-ball cub.
I rap his muzzled chin
and rattle peapod music in my hand.

My home could be branches and straw,
torn plastic sheeting balanced on sticks
may be nothing.
My home is my self.

I'm his fate,
calling the tunes of risky weather
scorching his throat to sand
or swallowed rain.

Punch-drunk shuffles
one paw to the next.
He manages a sluggish jump
dawdling sunglass people from their bus.

This is our limelight:
I hit - he dances.
They press their cameras
and slide the creased note into my palm.

For those who pay nothing
I wish them my fleas.
I nearly make a life,
and know the phrase for thank you
the word for please.

HAPPY FOR THE CAMERAS
(for Fikret Alic)

They say look fat. We do our best.
Fat and happy for the cameras.
If I smile they might pass over
ribs like the side of a broken ship.
It's not my skin anymore.
Only the thumbprints are mine.

Don't ask me what I've seen.
If I look happy hard enough who knows?
More soup more bread
lighter work tomorrow. They treat us well.
Why should the man beside me cry?
His stupid shoulders jolting.
What do tears mean? Goodbye soup goodbye bread.

Tonight I make a newsreel in my head.
We're meeting when it's over
somewhere safe
near a road where this can't happen again
because the road has gone, the country gone.
They ate its name.

I've finished with towns that survive as smoke.
I sleep thinking of my daughter
three months old when I left her
singing her own language
on her own tongue.

THE GIFT

Your parents are stooping above you
together because it's a dream,
arguments calmed by the gift they choose:
a series of boxes.

You open the first to find the second,
the second to find the third inside;
each time expecting this will hold your gift,
each one enclosing the next box and the next
until no smaller box could exist.

When you lift the last lid it's empty
and you cry, disappointed at the game.
What have they given, that fierce generation?
A diminishing sequence of boxes
hiding the gift of air.

MY FATHER'S STORY

When you said you once loved my mother
your brother's wife
you gave me back my birth
on a park bench under spinning leaves.

"Anything you want to ask ask."
So I did. Every detail.
Later you said I boned you like a kipper.

"I was engaged to a Jewish girl.
She died of cancer.
I was in a state so they took me in
and I abused it.
We were young. We knew no better.
I was selfish then.
Yes, it went on seven years
until he found us.
I want his forgiveness, and he never gave it;
now he's gone. Yes I know, I know
I should forgive myself.
I thought you were an ugly baby, honest.
When you came I thought you made me a man."

I've come to make a man of you again:
force you like a punishment
to tell your son your story
stung into each memory by my chant
"what then? what then?"

I held you when you cried,
while a police car patrolled slowly past us.
Two men in a cold park
comforting each other
are bound to be up to no good.

HIDEAWAY

I shadow you into a grove of lilacs.
We lie on mattress-moss:
your flecked head at my ribcage sinks and lifts.

If we stay embraced this way
nothing will happen.
If we pretend to sleep we can't be harmed.

You rise from me, a restless gull
to swoop against the giants
steepled like oaks around our hideaway.

Three years old, you can teach your father
after we fake sleep
it's time to fly the net and grapple light.

LIFTING MY SONS

They've had wet beds five nights running. It's time
to lift them both again before I sleep.
I whisper their names to wake them. They come
into my arms as if they trust their lives to me, droop
their dozy weight against my shoulder.
Each boy yawns at the toilet and pees. When I turn
to carry the youngest back I catch us in the mirror:
a father holding his son.
This glimpse of how I wanted it to be.
If I could become a father who gives love
and keeps his temper, not suddenly
lunging from quiet into screams. If I could have
known my father thirty years ago. When
I cry he'll be there, lifting me again.

SWIMMING WITH MY SONS

Weighted on either hip, like jugs at a well
I lower us into water.
Tingling with its element they yell
wet echoes. Our legs, six jelly-tentacles, waver
in the stir we make. I'm the only one of us
standing on the pool's cool floor.
I become their raft, and pass
each child from one hand to the other, before
the eldest tells me to hold tight.
I nudge their buoying bodies, slippy to lift
and slide into my arms. The light
here is a wobbling thread that will break and drift
together again. We shiver. They hang on like snow
hugs a branch, until the time is ripe to let go.

THE WATER-CHUTE

Beached here six years ago, drenched and newborn,
now he swims ahead of me, showing off.
He's under my skin. When we met at dawn
the first time he looked like me born again, as if
he could get it right where I went wrong.
Pure arrogance. He's not my second chance.
He's his own man, whose roots are loosening
like milk teeth, whose inheritance
spits blood. Now he wants to ride the water-chute
alone, poised at the top of wet stairs.
His skinny-whippet muscles strain this taut
leash between us. I bob among Sunday fathers
while he's gushing through that wide blind
tube. Splashdown. He's washed out at the end.

TEN DAYS BREAK

When you took the kids away for ten days
I thought Freedom! This is the life.
The house to myself, I bought drink and wrote as if
I hadn't touched a word for weeks. I worked each phrase
into the early hours, happy in ways
I missed. It brought back my belief
in living that dream. Devotion to writing: no wife
no kids no distractions. A fantasy that sways
through my years like a flame, fattening
or sputtering. By the end of the week it wanes.
These rooms look gutted, echoing
me to me. When I pick you up near the bus-lanes
all of you happy and talking at once, I'm juggling
kids and dreams of books with my name down their spines.

VIEWS FROM SIX WINDOWS

I feel ashamed to go naked about the world,
And am curious to know where my feet stand...and what this is
flooding me, childhood or manhood...and the hunger
that crosses the bridge between.

Walt Whitman from The Sleepers, 1855

THE HIGHEST ROOM

Looking down   through glass
white vines surround the conifer below.
It seems that thinly-bandaged tree
can't survive without them,
may even feel blessed.

If I'm a nested tree
scorched by autumn burnout   housing songs
I can't be lopped from what happens downstairs.
Cut the edge of a pasteboard man,
remove him and he hardly leaves a hole.

I want to be where the children's arms
bind like ivy round my shins and knees,
weighting   halting my walk
until I cradle a child to sleep
on my body's slow ride.

I've come so far it's brought me home
to a cramped desk at the window.
Words graft our lives together
piercing through the glass
onto this page.

BAY WINDOW

When night heads for your skin like a great dark train
you know
however much you throw your face back at a joke
downing wine with friends at the empty table
you know
night blacks you out like a match in a puddle.

Years I've paced this lightbulbed room
juggling four glass hoops:
career marriage writing children,
all the gifts that promised to complete me.
I smash one, crack another
clattering in a circle on the boards.

I don't know where I'll be next week, next month.
Scuffing grass beyond that hill
I might as well stay here,
almost safe   aiming to become
dried translucent honesty in a vase above the hearth
snuffed between the wind's thumb and rain's finger.

FROSTED GLASS

       ah   ah   ah
jump for air   who's drowning?
I wrestle in a water-sack
Houdini under ice
what do you do if you lose this bet
burst your lungs   forget to breathe?

       I jack-knife   nose-dive
         eye-holes in my head

What help are words underwater?
Waves rub their thumbs over tissue-paper skin:
one page nearer the knuckle
nearer the bone.
I thought dissolving into water
meant only winter death
and resigned myself to freeze here like a man.

       forgive the cold
        marbling my hands and heels

When I'm sliding down a sandbank
into twitchy sleep
nothing to hold on for, no-one to believe
I become that hunched-up child again
who grips your nightdress sleeve
         to keep him safe.

NIGHTSHIFT

2am
again
your nightmare cry
yanks me like an anchor
from the seabed where I sleep
lunge
a stumbled shadow
for the light sliced like a door into your room

I tap your back through cot-bars
hum and croon   it doesn't help.
I rock you like a father should
as if you're the wave and I'm the harbour.
Your fists and kicks
wrestle my awkward comfort like a dragon in your dream.

I'm on nightshift   fatherhood's backside
unable to quiet you or quiet myself.
Something's howling down these walls,
your gaping mouth a well I pour my care into
and cannot fill the brim.

You're eating me alive.
The father who thought his skin
could never scorch such anger's clamped inside it now
hammering to get out.
You're a door I need to break apart
barring me from calm.

When I hit
what taut strings pinion me
from being the man who hits and doesn't stop?
If I'm Gulliver love webs me,
one tense inch from drubbing you like a drum.

Nightblue curtains shut the moon outside.
Your window grids the prison lights
jabbing that hill   a circular chain in flames.
My fury lifts and sieves like smoke
above the blackened stacks.

Frazzled lad, lie still and let me hold you,
mend each other's temper in our arms.
I'll lull you in this hall light
until your lids tilt downwards
and I sink you into tussled sheets:
don't go dad   I'll stay till you're asleep
having peered over the edge of your hold on me
to the need, the rising cries
where a man's bound hand and foot
by a boy's love   raging.

                Within hours
your yell cracks my shell like daylight's beak
                thinking every morning
                it can't be time already
                where's my sleep

I part your curtains,
sag your pillowed weight against my arm
and we blink where dawn has blazed our view:
yellow on laburnum buds   white on lilac torches.
It snuffs the distant prison lights,
indistinct from hills like slated roofs.

Where does it hide   the chilling night between us?
Sometimes the answer echoes *inside me*.
How can we start to understand what happens:
know there's a place for night but this is day?
Waking you say "We love each other don't we?"
I give the right reply   we're reassured.
Dazed, we pause together by the window
pushing our love to its limits, and beyond.

MARRIAGE BED

We lie on a sheet cold as paper. How much
can two hands hold without pulling apart,
letting the light we try to clutch
wash away like wine?
If you're scared of sleep I'll watch
and make a story from our lives, to start
where a fox and your dream combine.

When we met my fox's tail flicked a line
between your trees. His paws dipped holes in snow.
If you define
the couple we were then
as older children, swapping histories as a sign
of trust, now we know
the fox has gone. We're simply a woman, a man.

My story drifts off, slow
as your breath in sleep. I ask
myself *why lie*, making words glow
like stones through slime.
For months it's been blow on blow
banging our heads together. Love's task
is to speak the truth this time.

You wake and say your dream.
I'm walking beside you
down the aisle of a street. In our prime

we're dressed in wedding clothes: your antique lace,
my dated suit. Would we mime
those vows today if we knew
all we know of each other now, lying face to face?

This high, the phone-wire taps
our window. We rise and see
the goldfinches again. One raps
a beak on the neighbour's branch. Its jittery mate
jabs at scraps.
They're free
as fate.

THE WINDOW AND THE WINDOWLOCK

If the window's half-open
a breeze can stipple the hairs on your skin
like pine-needles
rising, one after another.

If you close the window
your eyes still measure ripened wheat
your fingers flex their tendons to describe.

Each word's a boomerang
spun to the breeze
bruising the nub of your skull again again.

Unhook the windowlock
walk onto cloud
and know at least your words
can match your dreaming.

ACTS OF PARTING

ACTS OF PARTING
(for Cliff)

acts of parting   trying to let go
without giving up
> *Adrienne Rich from Contradictions: Tracking Poems*

PREPARATIONS

When you phone out of the blue
to say you'll soon be over
I yank tulips from a vase
drop petals every move I make.

They're dumped in the dustbin.
You're living as if you'll die,
the edge of each wrist-bone
like a blade.

Now the tulips are rubbish
I'm ready for you
in our pact of bitten tongues
and no reminders.

SPEAKING HIS MIND

"Call yourself a friend? You cut down on your visits.
I've got to phone to get you to come over.
Maybe you can't take seeing him, I don't know.
His lung collapsed two days ago. They didn't think
he'd get through the night. He's frightened, very frightened.
They said he might not come home.
I held his hand eight hours yesterday. D'you know what that's like?
He had a good night's sleep last night and that was four hours.
Can you honestly say your conscience is clear?"

THE BODY SAYS

The body says: Collapse a lung?
No sweat. I soldier on, easy as breathing.
Pepper shingles across the ribs.
What's a little pain between friends?
Cultivate a wart like an anemone
playing around the windpipe.
Could be beautiful if they didn't leak its name.
Cancer? I take it on board.
Even that word won't floor me.
As long as there's breath I never sleep;
though I'm conning him each minute, cell by cell,
stitching his last infection thin as a needle under skin.

AT THE BEDSIDE

There's a hothouse in your skin. I can't get inside
to sweat it out with you: feeling shingles saw
your ribs; an air-mask denting the bridge of your
pinched nose. When I hold your hand at the bedside
this minute and five years ago collide.
I'm in the night before
our first son: squeezing a sponge for
his mother's tongue; kissing her hair as she cried
and rolled. I can't take her place. There's no choice
but standing by at this great occasion. I stand
beside you now, with no birth to make the price
you pay worthwhile. We talk about birth and
the fight to get here, while the hard word we won't voice
circles round our heads, about to land.

THE DREAM

Confined to bed in hospital
where reaching the sink to brush your teeth
means hours after strapped to the oxygen-mask
you dream of walking through a supermarket
guiding your trolley, ticking a list
mundane and free.

WAITING FOR TRAINS

"He's got two months." We take the doctor's word,
passing its crumbs between us. You're left out.
Two months shut under our tongues. I could shout
it through the hushed ward, like the man we heard
ushered inside a quiet room to cry. This ward
is a station where we mooch about
waiting, checking the clock, chatting without
giving ourselves away. You're polite and bored
in the gaps between pain and sleep. "The sooner radiotherapy
starts the sooner I get out of here
the sooner I'll put weight back on and really
live again." The platform shakes; doors swing. It's there.
While we glance away momentarily
you climb aboard and leave us, miles from anywhere.

SCARED

"I bet that District Nurse'll douse herself in Dettol
when she gets back home.
I've seen people wash their hands
after talking to me.
Scared they'll catch something.
I'm the one who should be scared.
A cough or cold from them
could finish me off."

REMISSION

Now you know they can do nothing for you
you go home, walking out of hospital
as if walking is one of those beautiful
humdrum acts you reclaim, like standing in a queue
or using your own key. You're back in charge for two
months, ten, twenty. Anything's possible
when you talk like that. Risk it: be hopeful.
For weeks we watched a hyena chew
your fat, skinning you to the bone. Scratching a flea
it yawns and drops you now. It will let
you walk away for a while, plotting to be free:
"Listen. We'll go to London and send that
fucking doctor a photo of me
in a kiss-me-quick hat saying Not Dead Yet."

MUSCLING IN

Who does he think he is?
Sneaking up on two young men
oblivious, crouched together
planting snowdrops for next spring.

He's got no business here
muttering sweet nothings,
bribing you to leave your home
with promises of heaven.

Why isn't someone screaming?
If he gets away with you
there'll be no stopping him.
He'll root out anyone's daughter
anyone's son.

THE MOMENTS

Arm in arm with Andrew round the gardens
your wheelchair is ditched for a while. Reaching the lake
we take the piss out of writers who make
a fuss about timeless moments: when light sharpens
each grassblade, and our past and future burdens
lift like cloud. I step inside the grotto. A black
mask smirks and a dragon sneers. You shout "For Christ's sake
don't have a Moment!" While the growth hardens
each minute like this is a gift. Waking Andrew
for midnight feasts when the cough scrapes its knife.
Planning how to write back to a friend who
pretends nothing's wrong. Patiently telling your mum it's like
Andrew's your husband. Wanting to be two
old queens: surviving this, having the time of your life.

GOING TO THE SEA

You're not going to the sea.
It's too far. You'd be shattered.

You'll stay here. "I'm in pain.
I'm alive. It's better than nothing."

When you're ready for the journey
you could lose yourself in light
coming to that precipice, that sea.

EACH BREATH

A dull orange night-light. This underwater sound
bubbles from your oxygen-flask as if we're sleeping
inside a fish tank. I wake for your breathing
like I listened while the children slept and
feared each breath might be the last. We've planned
a rota for your nights and it's my turn. You're gripping
my hand. I'll hold on for as long as you want though you're slipping
away. Drugged and jumpy you ask "Do I take the road behind
me or that one over there?" It gets you down
when I misunderstand and say "Stay here."
Your cough's a tight gasp now. Each breath's drawn
like a half-empty bucket from your
shallow lungs. Each breath's thrown
to unlimited air.

PARTING SHOT

"Sod the afterlife.
When I'm dead I want to *be* dead."

to have to live
without your voice
in all this silence

BREATH

HERON

Killing time in a Clapham park on our last
drive down I saw a heron on the lake.
I thought it was a plastic decoy, fake,
until its beak jabbed and that black crest
quivered. I wanted it to fly, just
unwrap those great grey wings and take
off like an emblem over the park.
I waited. Nothing. Nothing but a heron stuck fast
in dull water while I waste time wishing
it away. The story of my life. I could jump and cry
out loud or drop these thoughts of flying:
let it stay for as long as it'll stay.
What about you? When I started understanding
each minute is enough you'd gone away.

THE GARDEN

After he died I cut down the trees.
I wanted as much light as I could get.
Stumps no fire could ash. The flesh of split
wood like clotted cream. I was up to my knees
in branches, finishing them off. In the breeze
made by all this space I wanted it
back the way it was. Dandelion clocks. Nettles. Thick wet
grass, and those over-ripe blackberries
squashed at the slightest touch. That garden's gone.
We'll rotavate, level and turf it. We'll
grow another garden where the kids can run
naked, like Eden before death. A year's over. I'm still
learning he's gone. Silence. Here's my breath. Listen.
Kids are laughing while this year's apples fall.

ONLY THE DEAD

Only the dead can say they'll never leave.
They've already gone, but return to you
at night of course, and some days you believe
they take your arm while you're cutting through
wet grass near a river. They say slow down
until you're walking by their side. You say
how much you miss them. The phrases blown
like their voice round your head are meant today
for comfort. Understand this. From now on
these are the only conversations you'll have.
You can love them all you like. You can
light candles in chapels, cry at night, rave
into thin air. The blunt fact of death
pumps your lungs, stuffs your mouth, rebounds like breath.

ACKNOWLEDGEMENTS

Acknowledgements are due to the editors of the following publications in which some of these poems (including some earlier versions) first appeared: *Acumen, Ambit, Envoi, Fatchance, The Frogmore Papers, Lines Review, The Observer, Orbis, Poetry Durham, Poetry Wales, The Rialto, Seam, The Spectator, Spokes, Sunk Island Review, Verse, Weyfarers.*

Lifting My Sons was a prizewinner in the 1991 National Poetry Competition and was published in the Prizewinners' anthology. *Acts of Parting* was published as a sequence in *New Statesman and Society*.

Walt Whitman's *The Sleepers* appears in *A Choice of Whitman's Verse* (1968), selected by Donald Hall, published by Faber and Faber. The lines from Poem 16 of *"Contradictions: Tracking Poems"* are from Your Native Land, Your Life: Poems by Adrienne Rich. Copyright© 1986 by Adrienne Rich. Reprinted by permission of the author and W. W. Norton and Company Inc.

Robert Hamberger and Blackwater Press wish to thank Marion Mathieu for the cover illustration.

Thanks are due to East Midlands Arts for a Writer's Bursary awarded in 1985.

Blackwater Press gratefully acknowledges financial assistance from East Midlands Arts.